"O Enkidu, what is this sleep that has seized you,/ that
and stopped your breath?": in Stephen Mitchell's rendition, Gilgamesh's ravished
incomprehension reaches out across millennia to grab us. Consuelo Wise's relentless and
stunning debut takes up a subject as old as written poetry itself. Or rather, she's taken up
by it, yielding a booklength confrontation with grief, grappling with the intolerable loss
of her brothers, and grappling just as exhaustedly, as inexhaustibly, with the limits of
language to express it. The result is profound enough to make praise beside the point.
On one page Wise crafts intimate, uncanny images with the precision of Alejandra
Pizarnik or Nelly Sachs: "the leaves fall softly on your not-/cheek"; "between grass
and language, mouth"; on the next, heart-rending plainspokenness: "they weren't parts
but that's how I remember them." She conjures a haunting and discordant music from
brackets, hyphens, ampersands, slashes. And boy's questions, like Gilgamesh's, remain
unanswerable; a book of tragic wisdom.

—John Beer, author of *Lucinda*

"See I lost two brothers," Consuelo Wise writes, "but once I begin, the boys—all the
boys—begin to merge."

Wise's debut book, *b o y,* is a meditation on loss and grief. *b o y* is two of Wise's own
brothers, and it is those boys she grew up with, or who didn't grow up, who were lost
to stunted opportunity and youthful recklessness, to speeding cars, alcohol, and the U.S.
penal system. They are boys with sisters, who grieve them, "& the mothers expecting /
the mothers // falling apart."

In Wise's tracking of sensation, memories return that resist understanding, and form
is continually made, continually falls apart. Yet Wise is unflinching in her effort to get
at something elusive and necessary. In poems where absence looms, *b o y* explores the
seemingly irreconcilable: how to let the dead go while keeping them close; how to accept
that the fragments of memory one is left with are both partial *and* whole.

Silence is integral to the effort to *get at,* and rich with resistances. Resonant recurrent
shapes burnish one another: the curve in the road that her brother did not make: the
animal circling before it lies down; the arm fitted around another's shoulder; one's cheek
against the dark. Wise's stunning syntax, in lines that tumble, undercut, and catch, creates
a form that holds grief, while in its fractures extends a singular beauty.

—Michele Glazer, author of *fretwork*

In *b o y*, Consuelo Wise creates poetic forms strong enough to hold the staggering weight of grief and supple enough to be remade by its force. Resisting the desire to make loss "smaller, less opaque," these poems are stricken with its large and layered presence. Never has a book of poems felt so much a collaboration with silence. These sequences are less scripts or performances than they are a kind of music heard within and against absence. Wise's writing is gorgeous, transfixing. As only the best poets can, she hears "not hereness." "We just want the feeling of coming up from that dark water—I do—/I want *that* feeling," she says. Even if these poems can't provide that particular solace, they make a language that takes us to something close to it.

—Mary Szybist, author of *Incarnadine*, winner of the National Book Award for Poetry

Cover art by Consuelo Wise

Cover design by Consuelo Wise
Cover typeface: Garamond
Interior design by Laura Joakimson
Interior typeface: Garamond

Library of Congress Cataloging-in-Publication Data

Names: Wise, Consuelo, 1986- author.
Title: b o y / by Consuelo Wise.
Other titles: b o y (Compilation) | boy
Description: Oakland, California : Omnidawn Publishing, 2024. | Summary: A
hybrid book-length poem in which the protagonist grapples with a great
loss. In this hybrid of lyric poetry and essay, Consuelo Wise utilizes
repetition, fragmentation, and syntax to construct a form that
repeatedly falls apart. Breaks in lines and fragmented stanzas are
followed by accumulative rushes, slashes, brackets, and words pushed
together. Throughout this book-length poem, Wise composes a meditation
and an investigation into loss and identity. Moving between sound and
image, aggression and subtlety, b o y pries open memories that resist
understanding but also refuse to be forgotten. Wise peels back layers of
mourning, considering how it can be experienced as a personal,
inherited, environmental, social, and historical phenomenon. Throughout,
the protagonist in b o y reenvisions ways to process a great loss,
listening closely and searching for words while "the earth is shaking
and the silence pressing down." -- Provided by publisher.

Identifiers: LCCN 2024002683 | ISBN 9781632431301 (trade paperback)
Subjects: BISAC: POETRY / American / General | POETRY / Caribbean & Latin
American | LCGFT: Poetry. | Essays.
Classification: LCC PS3623.I8236 B69 2024 | DDC 811/.6--dc23/eng/20240119
LC record available at https://lccn.loc.gov/2024002683

Published by Omnidawn Publishing, Oakland, California
www.omnidawn.com
10 9 8 7 6 5 4 3 2 1
ISBN: 978-1-63243-130-1

by Consuelo Wise

Omnidawn Publishing
Oakland California
2024

Contents

for my brothers

How to demand of composition that its contrivance come apart,
but leave the pieces intact?

how might I live death all the way to the edge of its form?

— Rusty Morrison

b o y

we buried you beneath the bombax
tree   not too
deep
          so you   could escape

the night
suited
          you

we carried you

up

          sky

     seeds of the bombax

     fall   tissue paper

     seeds

               iridescent   cells

    in the night
you call
               come

     see me on the table

see me   *now*

     tiger back   tiger
     climb

is that you
boy

your name became

your name   was   you   were
named

wind

the brother who burnt his leg on the motorcycle–brother who broke his teeth-out springbreak our parents split—skateboard to the front of the mouth—brother who pulled the tendon with the speedbag—hit the bag—arm stuck—hooked to the S curve—arm suspended. tissue out.
Older-brother-lift-him-down.

brother who seizure–liked-to-be-clean—wash clothes in bathtub—can't wait–laundryday. town. brother who racecar driver now—brother smoked cloves gave him/didn't want to/got sick/brother I push down—pavement*don't come with us*brother-who-money-who-care-for-us *me*

We grow apart from hurting.

Can't talk   don't talkmuchabout *him*stillmesister

boy

close though

brother-us.

the brother with records he couldn't listen to—no power-generator—brother reading stones
old stones—time-brother-made sisterme by
born first—brother-me punch in arm—brother who—bathroom—us get ready/school—use
same lotion—pluck eyebrows–brother who drunk at party—we don't talk /shy—brother
dad says made parents speak again—hospital—guatemala
brother my brother my older brother the brother I can't be to little brother—the brother
who—brother who—would you—brother of plants/on the plane—carrying cuttings in
pocket—brother-dad-who *my son*/ brother-who-with-hands   strong hands   *climb, hands*
 & holding cousins—sweep house-morning-wash dishes-mom-dad-not-home-chop wood &
food for us /brother-who-me-my-brother-brother-of-mine*wish*could*be*brother-who-

brother   move them there to there   take in pocket
               make grow. ofguatemala

boy

who doesn't won't not be

          build grass house   track
   jump   bike dirtboard kick-flip

dive   pond

          brother show brother how to   showing not showing

how not to

grow up

20

then, brother born
need you

       the brother who. brother.   doesn't speak   can't   doesn't   not /how we

brother stuck.   —say *blind.* brother who can't
—them say, *can't hear.*

born at home.   air-vacked.
       Hospital. ICU.

brother we feed sweet potato to and

walk around the house. the special-way-need-learn*how*
hold you.

      care for.   /I think he listened so carefully   made us

*hear*better

feeding tube. blend food. massage chest. hypertension. sweat.

*talk to*deep breath.

the brother with the golden hair   long lashes. brother with the wide eyes,
the flitting eyes.

Green rubber chair.   touch button, *tell us*

      little jewel mother*workedsohard*for
she wraps you in cedar boughs

[how gets/must
 get good at this] *bury sons*

all my brothers. my brothers.

the problem of following sounds, or, if I try to inhabit the form I imagine of him—

then also not wanting to speak and not wanting to name

—like that which is getting outside of, being apart from,
& losing it to talk about you—*stay away*

my little-you pressing forward

[there is also a storage jar in the painting, and an old man, a child, a young woman under the rock, and another woman beside the old man] I want the pieces to match up; the vessel that carries, the illustration, the figures, my brother beating the grass with the stick, the humming that comes out from the mouth to make the sound
of the weedwacker.

[the brother who-the brother who-the brother who-the brother who-the brother-who

brother

The earth is shaking and the silence pressing down.

—our backs, how we sleep in the grass

 Hold on.

[in one version there are sticks in his hair, in another—gasoline, we wait to call it—it's not homicide but there are boys in the dark on the curve & we do not know their names]

river

my brother goes to sleep and wakes up a real boy

[the others are carrying water, but you can see that the old woman's jug has broken and the water that is left in the sherd you can see she is pouring back into the jar]

vow, my little
you
                         not childof

summer
                       dried in bundles
    —by the bed
in the bed   *[be gracious to the dead, do not stab the dead]*

them-still-awake.   summer*you* forget

37

[the female figures above Pentheseleia are carrying water in broken pots]

I want you to be free, I do, but I'm afraid to lose you.

& the mothers expecting/ the mothers
falling apart

river of my

madeof   your*eyes*
upthehill—

water; eyes *so*
dry, water-them get so
watery, so dry.

my eyes of yours
ofmadeof

River. back.
Come.] *real boy*

[water in broken pots] of
& making you my tumbling outgrow
you   carryingof

boy; neck

[our mother is somewhere washing her hands]

whatever in front of me   contain-you   on the table   put you
         bedroom

                [no longer does your mother take you in her hands]
last slept in

blanket with the blue birds

   cedar boughs running down, all down

your back

            ocean

water filling up   out

     & into

I gather. cannot.   /this my short arms smaller than theirs
but was am quick & tidy /at these things   my-
my haven't you had enough/can't-get-no. please. *up please.*   The child still
asking, her not responding
the over & on the counter   climbing up the counter, sitting on

the counter.   small feet, holding

still.

Yes—now hold out your hand.   *[the necessity of burying the dead, and its crucial*
importance to the family of the deceased]

 [small bundle] get   [air] by

it's not having you made me

River of how & if long enough

            on the side of the
hill, if long enough

to make a mark.

Round pressed spot
where

the boy lay down—smooth grass.

How deer in the meadow below the orchard
got in]

river of you made of me   of
sister-*me*back.

I want to see the spot on the grass on the side of the hill where you crashed.

I want to see if the grass is pressed down.

[how you lay]

[Self Portrait]

memory or not
having them

to make or allow myself

a story; *night*—

the small windows
open

sound of rain

I am mother, little mother

—but you, you're not
my son. *Sing*—

down
all

the jeweled
bellies,

boys

the holding

in the neck

Ocean.

what filling
means without emptying

what blue is this—not blue of

 breathing.

       —into

night.

into brother.

soft—est
hair

mouth of listening

closed
door

a quiet house

quiet quiet

house.

[the silver pieces of your not-voice, your
not-breath—the shell being made
    how the ocean   *that these things cannot
exist in the same form,* can they—

        still you. born.   stars shaking
  the way they look when you look at them
hard.

us moving this way /little mother

working so hard
then, no-holding. no-hands. they take
you to breathe
  gloved hands shape you back

in, & *back*]

ways of making

[boy

                                   how many they lose

                                   & the boys,   eyes

                                   open in the dark
too open—open, to *stay open*

                                   & mother's careful hands

                                   not one, but *two*
                                    preparations,

                                   & the sound
                                   of softened metal colors   vanishing &

                                   nothing
                                   filling us
                                   up

———— window?

cannot
ofyou

wait   sleep, *mother*

darkness of skull, are you waiting

your
soft breath

against the pillow

                I am-I am, what shape am I?

boy,   cannot cannot

I see

you   follow my voice

grass, wind

[a state of waiting]

b o y

he drinks
        from the cold
pool

        runs   where   the black
cat runs   he's not
dead yet

        I ask the mockingbird
toucan   you-know-me

                        I can't remember
my name
or where   I came
 from
        or where   I was going

the small bundle   to get air by

Brother   the boy with the moon in the eyes

light in the bucket

I am trying to see you however I can,

                                    I open
first the door, looking through the dark metal

grate thru the door at the light

all the words in there for me, I think they

might, if I listen carefully, see me

let me see them

/how to remember you/ *how* what I get of / the leaves fall softly on your not-

cheek/shadows of mimosas on the sidewalk/ your not-back walking in front of me on

the path/ not-neck/ hair, legs.   all your not-ness of

/ I don'tcan't /*but still* am seeing/stepping softly

 we /don't wake up your brother/ wake brother/your not-hands doing the bundling/ your

not-back to me

 gathering dry blades. our brother reminds me you didn't have the same hands,

but now in my memory both strong,   wide   both good at making

things.

we're walking on the rocks   green river   below

ear   hands   cheek

Tonight the moon an empty
basket of eyes, an empty
mouth. I fill up the basket
& cannot understand
what words in there, what

big, big world.

My small ears for seeing,
my small eyes for hearing.
I am trying best
to understand
you—

We hang the clothes from the stairs, down then across the small courtyard above the pila, zigzagging to cover the most space. I like washing the clothes in the pila, filling one side with water, using the ridges to scrub the clothes. I like the motion of scrubbing.

Our tia sends us to the corner at lunch for the large glass bottle of Coca-Cola. We buy candy reaching our hands across the counter beneath the metal grate, choosing all the sour ones filled with goo to squirt in our mouths. Then run back quickly.

I should let the pink bombax
flowers fall

the seeds
dry up

I should let
the leaves gather beneath the tree

somewhere the black magpie
& howler monkey are shrieking

the wind is a hot
wind above

I don't stop long

enough to brace myself
keep

climbing

Talking about your not-hereness is a repeating process of negotiation—first I say *goodbye, let go,* say—*this last time*—then I'm speaking to you & again you're beside me, filling the air with listening.

It's 2017 and I am boarding a plane to Los Angeles.

I am boarding the plane to see you, you've been dead fifteen years I have all my bags packed pens, sticky notes, books, laptop, charger, hard-drive, two blank notebooks, camera, clothes, hat—

between grass & language, mouth

the grass in the mouth / words I try to get out

the barreling through

my brothers, my brothers, I'm ready to see you—

What my mother does to make Rowan heard
& still a year later when the friend says, *it seems so much longer since he died*

Something about facing—I want to say.

—my brother goes to sleep and wakes up a real boy

Ocean at the door, blue chest, our little window.

How the chest looks and isn't warm

be my eye, my tooth, my ears for seeing

even in death they make you unreal.

—little cavity for falling

I want to sleep in the dark world of your listening

how hard you tried

how an animal lies down, the resting
in circles happening.

my mother, why she is all days
pulling wet sheets from the bucket

See I lost two brothers, but once I begin, the boys—all the boys—begin to merge—

There was an accident. The one driving, the other arriving; the one hit the other, motorcycle
to the front of the car

the curve, always a bad curve—
but these weren't my brothers. The boys merge.

An act of holding, or knowing, is it how we look out for—each one part of the other, we
grew this way, attached as if to a line against the river bank, summer, us ready to jump

the line moving up then down as each boy
 dives.

It doesn't matter who
when the curve in the road bends toward the hillside
a ridge, a ravine

the coast another—
edge of the water against the sky.

Somewhere out there the boys are running, or us with our damp shirts, June *again*
& the ticks climb

dirtbikes on the road below and the sound of wingspan, vultures, light on the water—oak
leaves blowing against the top

of the water—how much time has passed—

Before before before   & maybe today
we'll see them—the eggs

their nests camouflaged spirals of rocks, where they lay them just slightly
beneath the surface of the sand. Rocks hot on our feet.

The bird limps, makes its sharp cry to stop us
we follow its thinning sound.

[I'm not going back because I want to be there, but to try and explain how it happens]

   little pressing forward

Rise then fall   shape of my arm to your shoulder.
Around the fire, bottles, rags, the rolling   the side of the hill.
Rattlesnake grass.

Smell of gasoline and—*where are you
now?*

How many times did you roll—how fast were you going—did you accelerate at the turn—

& the mothers expecting/ the mothers
falling apart

& the fathers—what of the fathers   fathers, where were you—

away

—Night,

what is it Guatemala, with your long green caress—

By the end of months I felt its shimmering back, following, was it—is it *just*

grass blown by wind   grass holding,

   concealing, shaking.

Place out of which to disappear us them

—It's hard to talk about you without the rest—

see, so many boys of summer, California, the hills ready
always, to burn

—and I'm not even talking about the girls—

Let me be clear—in every city, every town

down by the river, street, side
of the highway, gravel road, by car, drunk, falling

we're always losing you. And the day
turns to a year, then another. Grass dry, again *June*

I begin to see the buckets of water, hear them.

I'm looking for ways of finding
you

& I hear the words thin, and the sensation of
silvery grain.

b o y

doesn't
          speak

the language   I ask him
in

               offers me
 a pink orange with black
seeds

               cuts it
with a sharp
knife   colors

of the rocks

black
               silver   grey
spotted

               you
 were   named

                         lightning

he asks
          my name

hummingbird

pulling-up
moving*swift*   through cave

river   & out

of it—

African violets in the sill, thinly sliced persimmons
pressed against the window

to see through, & their seeds
like stars. A ring.

Frara jacha, the green wire of a climbing

philodendron.
some bones from a chicken in bowl.

jade pile. cleaning the grate.
her telling me to take the bottle of diluted bleach from beneath the sink and rinse the
sink

"the things good to do"

to do, that I learn from her—

mother, little mother

but she wasn't my mother,
grandmother

Suddenly fifteen years pass

what *take my time* means

I lose you over and over and get good at this.

I want to know you always, know you more.

—that you've been carrying him all these years

I cross the street, my hands full; it's summer, the woman on the other side waves me to
cross & I think, *rush*

then she's calling

take your time and the shadows of the maple are moving
and I still can't say—no,—I'm tired of speaking

I've been speaking so much.
I keep recalling the day you died

one day and then a year had passed and now
here we are again, *June*
and you're not-here in the chair by the window and your not-food in the bowl & Mom

what's she doing—

I'm always afraid to call.

June again—

Maybe it wasn't mother, maybe it was

Grandmother—why *she* all days
pulling wet sheets from the bucket

—the day I lost it taking care of her. I started screaming and crying,
how my life was happening to me.

I wasn't in control of it—how I'd-don't want to live that way, how-I wanted-to-be driver
 of my life/not letting things happen &

she with her dry erase board/sitting on the green exercise ball /she saying with her hand

and the dry erase board pen/ in the air
she saying *me too, me too*

her jaw shaking, how it set with the illness

she couldn't close her mouth easily
she'd choke if the liquids filled up her mouth and she couldn't get them out

soon enough—I acted like a child that day, embarrassed

a tantrum—I was afraid of losing myself or the hold on my life—I was afraid I was just
going to stay there in that place

And she, looking at me with her wide eyes
her no-voice, and her body shutting down—

All of us so angry—this short, sudden pull to get her away from us
she was only 67

and so healthy and I'm still upset
all the things I didn't

learn or say or get to tell her
because *Mother*, motherme

all days   I miss
the letting things

you   happen
—that we can't, or, don't

anything about

[What it meant that in my dream we both *were* Agnes Martin; saying, awake *am I envious that she has space?* Can I *just* write *about* space why I can't Why I'm having *these* mixed feelings **a w a k e** Why time is a boring concept & annoyed by having to engage with it over & over—my ongoing search *for you*   always talking to you time present and contained and spoke**n to** in every word of you

 I n t r u s i o n a l y s s u m *SPILLAGE* through 1, 2, 3, important deaths *this way* Isn't this how time movesHow I became overgrowth is what I wanted of you I'm tired of these thoughts but My family ~~is always~~ growing and getting cut back ~~about it~~, I'll outgrow you, *that* won't matter/ shaking ground cover What you meant by "sugar feeds infection" What you meant by *sweet bitter* What you meant by "immobile" What you meant by *wild*—what she meant by "strong mess" I heard **a s y l u m** A white fluffy ground cover, the first flower I ever learned. *Mostly white.* you precious mess *What the* state of this country Trying to get my friends to see the Guatemalan movie—GuatemalAlways there *for you* Hearing the whiteness of Portland 11 years I've, I'm became My youngest brother They shake with fear we'll GET~~ing~~ IN and "take take take" the lovely ground But I don't feel I can ~~differentiate~~ what you meant by "somewhat tangled gardens" What I meant by please. cover cover, **I-hear-you** me up   see, wake *brother,* you little silver thread— ~~This time~~ I see, remember, — understand, No, it's that all this—I've experienced before—am experiencing again, differentiate *you?* where are you-spot on your head remains soft till the cap grows over. don't you hear me— ~~fear of~~ press it out US **w h o** saying we love you we love youweloveyou *come back* no wind-blue-you no ground cover shaking *in the morning* the first star

carryingyou   stones in my palms steps   seeds falling around your feet
   in my hair jacaranda still blooming in your ears filling your ears -the-out-of-you-I-don't-
want   out of me, parts of carrying you   stones in my palms steps   seeds falling around

my feet   in my hair   jacaranda still
blooming

 in your earsfilling *your ears* with

listening purple blossoms-the-out-of-you-I-don't-want   of me parts of carrying you
stones in my palms*listening* purple inyourearblossoms

It's true I don't ask for, am not asking for clear answers. I don't expect that, the ocean today was not the ocean I expected to run into, or it's that it was wilder than I wanted going into it, for it to be.

ocean was green today, the waves broke, I couldn't measure

them. do you want to talk to me about all of this inside my body, in every part of my body, —as I tell my friend I try to stand, both legs apart to hold myself, steady.

there are persimmons in the bowl from uncle jim, oranges on the table she brought me, marigolds with eucalyptus from my birthday. I was missing you and you looked from the photograph out.

you—the first time
all this time, who
I've been talking to.

do you know what that means?

I can't remember how old we were
it was late at night, we were visiting a friend of dad's in the santa cruz mountains and the small windows, open.

I've tried to explain this—how the pulling happened, the night getting in with its wide, dark strides—what they were—broad leaves, they pushed against the air in the room, light speeding time apart—what that meant.

it doesn't mean what they say it means. I think of the green bird with the long green tail—jacaranda, bombax, silver seeds falling and the butterflies filling up out of the river.

we walk for a long time without speaking.

there are still reasons I want to apologize, but now it's been fifteen years I've been alive,
not you—

they try to tell me about growth but lately I've been thinking how you,
moving them there to there to there—watering & moving quickly; the whole time they were
growing & outgrowing

their pots. you kept replanting them.

I'm not surprised by the things you do.

why should I be—I've known you forever.

—when we were kids—we were only
ever, kids—

I see the leaves press the window,   all they want is out
& you—*you?*

it doesn't make sense
but I think of every
thing, who you'd love—what you'd do, how you'd feel about

—I didn't ask because I thought—or could never—one can/never think

stop—you're bothering me, I'm trying to do something
get out—all the words to you
—for you.

I spend so much time thinking how the words look

how much is left

between us. the words hold together.

I come up with other words for body   but all I think is
body.

what it looks like when it turns
to ash in your hands and you put your hand in it, grab it
throw it.

again, how bad I learn things—why it's so hard when it was—but it wasn't easy (for you)

I say untrue things and feel sick
like what if all I'm saying is just to keep myself together
because really I want to let everything

—get out of me—

but this is really what's untrue

all I'm trying to do is
—I don't want everything to dissolve between me & the world and get lost in it

this second time around   I
throw you

eucalyptus   pine   orange,   my windy eye
I ask your hands,   put flowers   in our
mother's hair

b o y

the lights move
around
                    the room

    dim

                    the boy tells me
they're fireflies

    we know this
    isn't
    true

    how old
    are you

    my name is wind

     he says
              I'm tired

    can I stay   here

                    I think it's ok
      I say
he must ask

    the people
                    in the town

but I think

                they'll say

      yes

            as I say this   I know

I'm wrong

in the pit   where the taro root
grows

             it's hard   to swallow

 the boy says he won't
hurt us
         I tell him

he-better-go

                 he tells me
how long he's been

walking

           I cannot understand

four   ten   twenty-one six

forty-nine

           I leave the room

outside
no blue   in them

no blue or
green

I run back
to the room

the boy is lying there

I think he's sleeping

the room tells me
what's happened

look what you've done

Kioma & Alejandro and Rowan

my three brothers.

it's hard for to me to explain how these boys relate

I don't want them to all be connected so simply

but it seems true— these boys with their soft hair,
their strong listening.

we were this way.

listening
in the dark we moved, silently.

we moved so many times.

I spend a long time filling and unfilling the buckets.
they don't, I don't remember if they existed until now—
vessels carrying something—what?

where we took our baths, how we

sat in the bath.

the bath where the one brother washed his clothes
he was only six.
he liked to be clean.

The bath where the other—the youngest, bathed with someone holding him
above the water, deep breaths,
his muscles relaxing.

What is this I'm making, that may or may not have happened—
something I can't know
that I'm trying, is it

just
waiting
asking /I ask you

the two boys, one of them—you, the other—my friend
the one who hit the tree with the car.

In the dream we're in the grocery store, you won't look me in the eyes, but you look back
once & your hair   a fine, dark sheet.

you can't for some reason
talk to me
don't know
me—don't see
me or *can't*

the other boy does / & he gives me a hug and

I hold it all morning.

what will you do with this thing,   shell
in your hands

it seems important for me to deal with this part   the hands

what the hands do

I'm taking my time   walking on the beach

I stop looking for you   you're everywhere but you don't see me.

I have been looking for you with your little hooves   whatever *that* means
beneath the water   when I want to see you/ when I am walking or   awake in the dark

is it easier to talk about you
—this way.   I risk nothing and you, you—

I'm afraid of this long strand of shells, how it's hurting me

how it keeps me under
it would be easy to say, *water*

& were that true

what would that/ does that mean—the stones are hollow inside, the shells hollow
the boys with

their soft shells, ripe for eating   see, everything I'm making

a cylindrical space, empty inside, or *that* is what it is

feels empty

or air that means nothing, feels like, looks like, smells of

is that you   your new

youness

I want something round   to round you out
that must be something I want
to do

because over & over again, I'm making
the thing— smaller, less opaque

it begins to feel simple, a few stones in my pocket

b o y

we go see
the baby

  his plumes
shake a torrent   we
name him
so

  he's a girl

        I have no hair left
no in me

        & the wind is shaking
the baskets in the trees
their

  seeds fall   butterflies from the river

    its green
blue
 all its color
          no more

in them

                  every city
air pressed   out

        every town

on the phone my mom tells me she's putting rocks in buckets

rocks she collects at the beach & along the smith river, the applegate
all over,—she's always carrying them

one in each hand, she balances the weight

large river rocks for her garden
or small ones from moonstone or agate beach

I'm collecting for mosaics, I just need to learn how to make them, she says

buckets I imagine, we used for washing, sitting, for gathering fruit, carrying
they're only partly true—they became

somewhere between the giant iridescent seeds falling in tikal & washing our kid bodies in
hawaii & not burying kioma but holding on to his ashes for more than a decade

because we don't, *not in our family*—is this true—

we don't bury ourselves.

everything on the surface for everyone to see, or the facts are, but the rest

the rest is a surface I keep

between us

parts in the hospital on the table

they weren't parts but that's how I remember them

the parts become as if separate from the whole

how time or memory separates them—gives them their new name

right ear hand cheek

in the huntington gardens with ursula and caitlin

I gather the pink blossoms of the african tulip tree

c and I reach up and pull the branch down, she's taller than me, I want the pod

shaped like a boat

my grandmother made a paper boat and slipped a picture of kioma as a three year old
in the boat, it's on the fridge

every time I'm home I look at it.

and the buckets keep spilling
or their water rests, trembling on the edge

our little you pressing forward,
the moon about to show its face—further and further you are
from us

the pink blossoms press & dry and lose their brightness, but there's still a tinge of purple
pink and the gold rim of the petals and the tiny hairs
and the pod on my dresser is fuzzy and golden and inside it,

you

I don't write for weeks, nothing to say

how do I say I'm tired of holding?

I don't know how to put this down, how to stop scrubbing, I don't know how to
let you
my mother, sister, little brother, my father
myall-of-us—how to pour the/wash the/bucket the/ let dry, there's no space between the
one and the other
surface I've been ignoring, there's no—space, I'm talking to my friend, he's asking me if I'm
experimenting and I don't know if I am
—have I stopped—

trying, *wanting* to try new things   my

image of you already
contained

my image of me the same

the form of this between a strand and a wave, a line moving from the edge of the eel river as
all of us jump, as all of us—some climbing with their hands in the divots of the cliff,
alejandro at 8 then 12 and 18 & 24 and the days between us since the first backflip and the
arms sweeping out

kioma and all the boys taking their leap against all of the almosts of *don't* and *careful* and the
heaviness and fires and what aftermath looks like or feels in the air

115

and how we, just trying to break/to cool/come up
from

it makes me think of the sheathes of dry grass stacked back to back/of each other

their perfect form. rattlesnake grass shaking.

all the blue nights of summer. all the pressures of now eclipsed by the fullness of the night
we lay our backs to

we just want the feeling of coming up from that dark water—I do—

I want *that* feeling

but in it is the same one of barely being able to—

water in my lungs, getting my face wet & how *fast* it dries—of all the ways I try to not
remind myself or just soothe

—*face of you*

what it feels like; waking up, remembering

oak leaves on the surface of the water, end of summer

yesterday, two days ago—a year ago—five years ago—fifteen years ago—yesterday
tomorrow because of you–because of/ you/my
our little jewel of moon boy and boat and august meteor shower and
my sisters' boys and my friend's baby and the water on our faces

[how to bring you home]

child me morning of

the world tells me my brothers, ~~with their soft hair~~

~~my brothers,~~ with their strong listening

memory tells me I am

shell, little shell ripe for eating

don't let them   ocean

 hear you   *don't* oceaning out   step

carefully   little
shell of

[boy sister me

I think maybe I lost myself

for hours this way,   till hours grew
to weeks and years

and all the time it's been since you were
here. I can't remember when I say, where I was going

I can't remember where I was going

what is this thing/is it something I can/not finish and won't my little bird of love I have for you because I am always trying so much to be part of you and want you back and want also to be free of

how a shell forms in the ocean   turning over   I keep
thinking how hard you listened

with your whole body   hear the world
hear the world not   see you

I keep thinking how little how much little we know

my brother with your cheek against the dark

Notes & Acknowledgements

The italicized brackets in the poem, "the problem of following sounds", are from *Sources for the Study of Greek Religion*, by David G. Rice and John E. Stambaugh. Words were pulled initially as an exercise to write and avoid thinking too much about what I was writing. Pulling words at random from books in my room, using a timer with various increments of time, I wanted to follow something unknown, intuitive and perhaps more physical than mental.

In the poem, "[What it meant that]", the Guatemalan movie I am referring to is called *Ixcanul* by Jayro Bustamante. Flickers of other voices include my grandmother, Agnes Martin, Karen Green, Sappho via Anne Carson, and heard, experienced or read racism and violence in news regarding immigrants and Trump's campaign to build a wall between Mexico and the United States.

The poems titled "b o y" came about in a number of ways. One began in response to a 2015 NYT spreadsheet that showed the various assault weapons used in US mass shootings with captions explaining the number of people wounded or killed. The numbers in one of the "b o y" poems correspond to the numbers of people shot and killed.

*

The majority of these poems were written in my second year of graduate school after the death of my youngest brother, which was two days from the anniversary of my older brother's death. I am deeply grateful to my friends and family for sharing many conversations, walks, meals and hard moments.

Michele Glazer, for challenging me to describe my brothers, for recommending poets whose work were guides, for teaching me tools to make these poems. Your care and mentorship have been critical to me.

Thank you, John Beer and Leni Zumas, for your kindness, insight and care. Our classes were rigorous and meaningful, they sustained me. My cohort and graduate community, I learned so much from you. Thank you for sharing a transformative time together. A special thanks to Kellie Cook, Jenessa VanZutphen, Alice Hall, Darla Mottram, Shane Van Hayden, Erin Perry, Steph Wong Ken, and Jon Krill, rest in peace friend.

Mary Szybist, thank you for believing in me and encouraging me. For my first poetry courses and your guidance over the years.

Eliza Rotterman, Darla Mottram, Sofia Theodore Pierce, Marina Mitchell, Ella Street, Ursula Berg, Charity Yoro, and Sonja Myklebust— for serious talks and artist fellowship at various stages of this project.

Karolinn Fiscaletti & friends at *Old Pal*, I am grateful to you for publishing my first poems, among them pieces of *b o y*. Kevin Latimer & *Barnhouse Journal* for bringing me out to Cleveland and organizing an incredible night at *Mac's Books*; for grieving and celebrating together.

Emily Bernstein, Simon Metcalf, and Lenny Bernstein for meals, coffee, fires, dancing. Sharing a very special home. You helped keep my spirits up.

To Anna Hoone, for going back in time and remembering with me.

Caitlin Ducey, for lending me your studio the summer of 2017, and for our early collaborations which gave me confidence in building a practice and slowly sharing my work and thoughts.

To my Southern Humboldt friends, and our young selves—and for the Eel, Mattole, Sinkyone and other resting places of our adolescence— in these poems some of us who aren't here are.

Kioma, in dreams and in waking life, and in my first words must be you — born first and always my big brother. Alejandro, Chenoa, Nayena, Adriane, Olivia, and Rowan James Morningstar, I love you.

To my beautiful mother, Karina Wise. For teaching me about poetry, in life and through grief, friendship, beauty, your curiosity.

To my father, Carlos Perusina, for teaching me how to talk to spirit, to be alone, to travel, if not always in reality through story at four in the morning with a cup of coffee.

To my grandparents, Susan & Frank Wise, for inspiring me to read and write and study, for your generous nature and insistence that we think and question and care.

Laurel, India, and Cord. For being there, and shaping me.

Y a mi familia Perusina Rivera, y a Guatemala por siempre, con todo mi cariño y amor. Y a mi Tia Tuti, mi abuelita Coni, and my ancestors who I feel in spirit and when I walk up the mountain.

Rusty Morrison, my heartfelt gratitude for inspiring me with your words, and for seeing *b o y*, and choosing to publish it. Thank you, Laura Joakimson, for your care and labor in making this book come through, and my deep thanks to Omnidawn.

Consuelo Wise grew up in Northern California. She currently teaches at Portland State University.

b o y
by Consuelo Wise
Cover art: Consuelo Wise
Cover design by Consuelo Wise
Cover typeface: Garamond
Interior design by Laura Joakimson
Interior typeface: Garamond

Printed in the United States
by Books International,
Dulles, Virginia on Acid Free Archival Quality Recycled Paper

Publication of this book was made possible in part by gifts from Katherine &
John Gravendyk in honor of Hillary Gravendyk,
Francesca Bell, Mary Mackey, and The New Place Fund

Omnidawn Publishing Oakland, California
Staff and Volunteers, Fall 2024
Rusty Morrison & Laura Joakimson, co-publishers
Rob Hendricks, poetry & fiction editor,
& post-pub marketing
Jeffrey Kingman, copy editor
Sharon Zetter, poetry editor & book designer
Anthony Cody, poetry editor
Liza Flum, poetry editor
Kimberly Reyes, poetry editor
Elizabeth Aeschliman, fiction & poetry editor
Jennifer Metsker, marketing assistant
Katie Tomzynski, marketing assistant
Kailey Garcia, marketing assistant
Rayna Carey, marketing assistant
Sophia Carr, production editor